Pre-K Phonics
Conceptual Vocabulary
and Thinking

Brian P. Murray

Introduction to Pre-K Phonics

Reading is the single biggest factor in academic success. Phonics is a proven method to accelerate the process of learning to read, and it will create much more capable readers. But that's just the starting point for this innovative course.

Vocabulary alone is a strong predictor of academic success, accounting for roughly 75% of the score on cognitive skills tests used to select children for gifted and talented programs. Cognitive researchers have known for over 100 years that all cognitive skills are at work during the process of learning to read. Children who grow up in an environment characterized by profuse verbosity and rich vocabulary gain an advantage in language and reading.

Pre-K Phonics is the perfect opportunity to tackle all of these goals at once.

To meet these goals, Pre-K Phonics doesn't stop at the level of "cat", but continues with advanced words in the phonetic range of a young child. Starting with Lesson 3, definitions, comments and suggestion are included in each lesson for the parent to facilitate discussion. Later in the workbook, words are presented that hold a cognitive payoff, including degree, shades of meaning, double meaning, and more. Finally, math and sight words are included to provide a final boost for accelerated learning. Given the age of a child, there is no need to hold a pencil, but thinking and imagination are required.

Parent's Guide to Pre-K Phonics

The key requirements of success in this phonics program are this book, a Word Board, index cards and sticky notes, and the beginning of a strong reading program.

The Word Board might play an important role in your child's education for the next 3 or 4 years. Clear your refrigerator of any papers, stickers, and magnets. Write the word "CAT" on a sticky note and stick it on your refrigerator. You now have a Word Board. You can also use a wall or a large poster board with the words "Word Board" at the top.

The index cards will help your child to transition from pronouncing individual letter sounds to pronouncing letter clusters and words. When you are nearly finished with a lesson, after the child has read through it once or twice, write each letter that you see in the lesson on half an index card, in a font large enough that when the letters are put together it's clearly a word. Mix up your cards. Read the words and invite your child to spell each of them. This exercise will be useful for the first 20 lessons, and for "silent e".

The reading program is going to require a bit of planning and organization. The local library contains an enormous curriculum of knowledge and skills for your child. Unfortunately, the curriculum is all mixed up, filed randomly, and most of the good books are already checked out. You need a strategy.

Learning some of the skills of an academic coach will help. Coaching skills are not complicated, but may require change in attitude and approach. The short summary of academic coaching is this: create the proper learning environment and let your child do the rest. The longer version is below.

When To Start

If you start too early, the first lesson might take 3 weeks. If you start later, the first lessons will go more quickly and you can zip along until it gets more challenging.

If you are not sure that your child is ready to begin reading, get a set of word blocks and practice word sounds. When your child has memorized all of the letter sounds, or at least the key ones, you can go to the next step.

Occasionally, you can line up the C, A, and T blocks and see if there's any recognition. I started this process at about age 3 ½ with high expectations. Every few nights, I would present the letters my son knew and add one if he didn't forget any. Alas, it wasn't until 6 months later that he was ready to begin with phonics. We began a month early anyway, and the first lesson took 3 weeks.

The Reading Program

Your child is going to develop their reading skills and a love of reading by reading books. This workbook will accelerate the process. Reading should be at least an hour a day, although if you are constrained by time, 30 minutes of this might be your child sitting alone sifting through books. If you can manage 2 hours a day, at least on the weekend, do it. This investment will pay off a million fold.

There are three key elements of a reading program. The first element includes the books that you enjoy reading to your child or books that your child wants you to read to her over and over again. Think of Good Night, Gorilla by Peggy Rathmann or The Hobbit by

J.R.R. Tolkien. Jim Trelease wrote the handbook on reading to your child called "The Read Aloud Handbook", which I highly recommend. It describes not only how to read to your child, but why the activity is so important.

The second element of the reading program is a set of books that your child can read on his own, step-by-step, starting with really easy material and gradually getting more challenging to match the growth in your child's skills. This is officially called a Controlled Reading Program, and no such thing exists in the United States for beginning readers. I describe how to put together an ad hoc controlled reading program below.

The last element of a strong reading program is a stack of random books that you picked up at the library at your weekly visit. Looking for fun and engaging books that you and your child can read together. After a few months of doing this, you'll probably just be looking for any book you haven't seen before and dropping it in your bag. In my experience, you can't judge a book by the contents. I mean not only that you can't judge a book by its cover, but even paging through the book won't help. Some books work really well for your child, some don't, and the only way to find out is to take the book home and read it. Any book that either of you select could be a winner. If your child wants to read a book, it's the most important book of all.

While you are pulling books off the shelf, you'll find books in a beginning reader series with a level printed on the front. These will be the basis of your somewhat controlled reading program. The actual reading level of any of these books will usually have nothing to do with the level printed on the front. It appears to me that the publisher took books from various authors, put it in their "Early Readers" series, and stamped a random level on the cover. Even with a book that is pretty close to the right lexical score that works for your child, half of the words could be at a year away. Unfortunately the lexical scoring scheme is not your child's lexical scoring scheme anyway, but an average of children who are not your child.

Some of these beginning reading books were a lot of fun to read, regardless of level. Most of the time, I just read the book and invited my child to contribute based on his level of reading skills. In the beginning, his job was to read a single word from the book, hopefully one he had seen from phonics, but certainly one with letters that he could sound out. Later, he had to read a single word from each page. Near the end of the phonics course he was in charge of reading every other page, with help, provided the book was close to his level.

In the course of bringing home leveled readers each week, I started to keep a list, marking which titles seemed easy and which ones I should save for later. I had a list for each publisher, and searched the library's catalog for each series to complete my list. When your reader is ready for a whole book, probably one with 50 words or so, go back to the library to retrieve books from your list and invite your child to read them. Repeat until all books were checked off of the list.

Harper Collins has a series called "I Can Read", with five levels. Their web site assigns a reading level from A through P. This series has over 500 books, so your library should have quite a few. There are 35 books about Biscuit the Dog and Danny the Dinosaur that are great for a beginning reader, and Berenstain Bears and Amelia Bedelia for an advanced readers. Frog and Toad, Paddington, Splat the Cat and Pete the Cat are good books for reading if you get them late in the process, or Read To if you get them early. There are 5 Flat Stanley books on this list. The Flat Stanley is a 2nd or 3rd grade series best saved for that age group. The Harper Collins series, minus early versions of chapter books, made up the bulk of our Ad Hoc Controlled Reading Program.

DK has board books and a beginning reading series. DK also publishes more advanced books on a variety of topics like Knights and Egypt. All of their books appear to me to be under the heading of Science, History, or Geography. We had a stack of the advanced DK books in the house at all times. We read the Knight book so many times my son memorized the definitions of words like "gauntlet", "crenel", and "merlon". Crenel and merlon weren't actually in the book, but since there is a word for everything, we did a research project to find all of the words for things on a castle.

Scholastic has a series called "Hello Reader" with over 200 books at the Pre-K level. There are some great titles in this series, like "I Spy" and Hello Kitty, but most are standalone books. The Scholastic web site provides lexical measures which I found to be very unhelpful. Again, whatever the way a lexical measure is calculated, it wasn't based on the reading skills of any child I know. Instead, if a word is near the grasp of your child, she reads it, else you read it. Some kids will enjoy the standalone books, some won't.

Random House has 582 books in their Step Into Reading Series. While Dr. Seuss can be found among their titles, most appear to be branded characters. We read the Thomas the Train series before phonics, but once we discovered the wonderful world of non-branded reading, we didn't check out many books from this series.

Simon and Schuster's series is called Ready To Read with hundreds of books. Except for Olivia (best books ever) and Eric Carle, I don't recognize any of the books on this list. Publishers have been very aggressively buying the rights to books to put in their beginning reader series in the last few years, but the characters in this series seem to have been invented more recently.

It is the duty of each parent to check all of these books out to find a few good ones that work for their child. Good books will show up in your home either because you put random books in your bag during a trip to the library or you were methodically checking books off of your list of beginning readers.

Leveled readers and random books were not the big winners of our trips to the library. The award goes to the picture books. The first trip to the library will likely uncover a book with the Caldecott medal, awarded to American illustrators. These are wonderful books. I find the books that have won international awards to be even more fascinating. There is the Biennial of Illustration Bratislava award, the Kate Greenway Medal, the Hans Christian Andersen Award and others.

Starting with a list of illustration award winners for the Hans Christian Andersen Award going back to the 1950's, I searched for books by author in our library catalog. Then I proceeded to get every book illustrated by these illustrators, mainly by placing holds and interlibrary loan requests. It took over 2 years to complete the list. This body of work is amazing. The whole family enjoyed reading these books and reading became the favorite activity of the day. Many of these books had quite complicated and tricky themes and needed to be read (or viewed) repeatedly.

By the end of Kindergarten, my child was reading each night on his own a book that is very advanced. Phonics laid the necessary foundation for this achievement. Practice with leveled readers was the bulk of the effort. The phonics work was critical, but this achievement could not have happened if reading wasn't fun. A steady stream of picture books from award winning authors guaranteed a continued interest in books. Award winning illustrators tend to work with award winning authors, and thereafter we've never been challenged to find a great book to read.

The Word Board

The Word Board will play vital role in your child's education and the development of your coaching skills. There are different types of words presented in this book, and the Word Board is used differently for each type.

The first type is basic phonemes and rules that your child will need to know in order to read independently. "Raw" and "jaw" are words of this type. When you begin Lesson 20, which includes these words, you can put one of these words on the Word Board if your child is struggling to pronounce these words. Lesson 26 introduces the silent "e", so you might put "mad" and "made" on the board if this helps.

Next, pick words that spur your imagination and put these on the Word Board. The words in bold font have important concepts for the imagination, name things that are usually unnamed (like sash or hull), or have synonyms of degree (like grasp or grin). Any word can be a Word Board word if it is new to the child, hard to read or remember, and it appeals to your imagination or your child's imagination.

If a word strikes you as boring, don't put it on the Word Board. "Raw" appears in Lesson 20 in bold. If you aren't really excited about the difference between raw and cooked, put something else on the Word Board from Lesson 20, like "wand" or "sack". On the opposite page, starting with Lesson 3, in smaller font, I include commentary with definitions for not only the vocabulary words, but other words that you might not be able to quickly define for a 4 year old. I prefer "sack" to "raw" for the following reason. "Raw" is the opposite of "cooked". This is starter thinking. "Sack", on the other hand, is different than a bag or a pack, and coming to terms with the differences is a lot more challenging. That is why synonyms hold more cognitive load than opposites.

Any word you come across in reading that involves a lengthy discussion can go on the Word Board, as well as any word you come across while researching images to define a word on the internet.

A couple of times a week, you can drag your child in front of the Word Board and invite the child to read, act out, or respond to each word in some appropriate way that indicates recognition. The demands on a child to cite the definition of each word are modest. An adequate definition may be a gesture or stating the word and its opposite with a knowing look. If the word is "grim", a facial expression is appropriate, usually with lots laughing as the parent calls out "sneer", "frown", "shock", "surprise".

Words that are part of phonetic learning and sight words stay on the board until the child can read it quickly in at least two consecutive trips to the board. The Word Board may fill up over time, especially with sight words. You may end up with 100 words on the Word Board. They will eventually all come down.

How To Teach Thinking Skills Like An Academic Coach

While your child is learning, there is a lot going on in his brain and numerous skills are being developed. At this stage in your child's academic career, you don't have to worry about a technical list of cognitive skills. Your primary mission is to support the core learning skills with the appropriate coaching skills. Here are the core learning skills that your child needs to develop in the next two years:

1. Reads a question thoroughly. Thinks about the problem. Reads it again. Looks carefully at odd or unusual terms or relationships. Ponders questions.

2. Gets the wrong answer and tries again with no frustration or anxiety.

3. Has a strong working memory.

4. Has a rich vocabulary.

These are the skills that you will foster during phonics. These 4 skills are prerequisites for a solid academic career in elementary school. These skills are also critical for a high score on a cognitive skills test, not to mention AP Calculus. The next level of skills rests on this foundation, and a child with the core skills will naturally pick up the more advanced skills.

Your job as an academic coach is to provide an environment that fosters these skills. This comes naturally to some but not all parents. Sitting next to your child for a 15 minute session that takes 45 minutes when your child is crying and getting the same word wrong over and over again and forgetting what you just said 30 seconds ago can be very frustrating. It's also very normal and part of the learning process.

A child will learn to patiently explore a concept only if the parent is able to sit there silently and wait. A child will learn to accept wrong answers as a necessary part of the learning process and try again repeatedly only if the parent is happy with wrong answers and sits their encouragingly waiting for the next attempt.

Working memory is a skill that the child will develop by mental exercise. It is more of muscle than a skill. The absence of working memory in the learning process results in frustration for the academic coach and makes 15 minute session take 45 minutes. My approach with children of all ages who have a working memory deficit is just to resign myself that a 15 minute session will take 45 minutes, and depending on the age of the child, it will take 6 weeks (for younger children) to 3 months (for older children) to get back to 15 minutes.

The absence of working memory manifests itself in a child who forgets the first word of a sentence by the time he gets to the period, or the child who forgets the first part of a two part question as soon as both parts are asked. Learning to read at a young age is a great way to build this skill.

There is an interesting process going on with beginning readers that makes identifying working memory strength more complicated. A child who just struggled through "put" the first time may look at the word seconds later and have forgotten how to pronounce it. This child is focused on the process of sounding out the letters to produce this word, and while the child is learning this process, the child doesn't see "put" each time, but instead sees "P", "U", and "T" that needs a mental process to translate. It can be even worse with the word "the". Let this process unfold, because what is unfolding is a thinker, not a knower, the long term results will be much better.

Since your child is so young, you have to worry about a 5th skill: Executive Functioning skills. Executive Functioning skills including setting goals, planning, and staying on task. A child who sits still and pays attention during an hour of reading, or does a puzzle start to finish, or plays quietly alone for an hour building something is demonstrating a high level of Executive Functioning skills.

Fortunately, an hour of reading every day builds these skills. There are other ways to like projects, games, puzzles, and art of any kind.

A rich vocabulary isn't a skill but masks a set of other skills. A child's vocabulary is almost as good a predictor of academic success as a formal cognitive skills test. Test makers know this, and vocabulary is a thread that runs through these tests. A new vocabulary word activates at least a half dozen skills in a child's brain. It's not just the fact that a strong thinker can be identified by of the presence of a rich vocabulary, but the process of obtaining a rich vocabulary most likely created the strong thinking skills. Similarly, this course is not designed to present advanced vocabulary to gifted children, but to create gifted children by presenting them with advanced vocabulary words.

If your child learns these core skills, directly supported by your approach to academic coaching, subskills will emerge on their own when your child is ready. If you are prepared to give your child as long as he needs to read a word, as many tries as he needs to get it right, provide patient encouragement even in the face of whining and crying, and give your child an opportunity to think about a new word or answer a question while you sit there in silence for the next 20 minutes watching your child think, then go directly to Lesson 1 and get started.

If a child has mastered the high level skills like working slowly and carefully and being prepared for mistakes, the child will teach themselves the more detailed skill set that is the target of GAT tests and differentiates top academic performers from the average. In the following discussion, I present the coaching skills in more detail within the context of this phonics book.

How To Use This Book Lesson By Lesson

The recommended pace is 20 minutes 4 times a week. The first lesson could take 3 weeks, but the goal is to get to one lesson a week about the 20th lesson.

During the first 3 sessions with each lesson, the child can read the words, and when ready, read the sentences. On the fourth day, the child can reread lessons for mastery. On the last day of a Lesson, the child can do the index card exercise.

The pace will vary with each child.

Lesson 1

The first goal of phonics is to get from C – A – T to CAT. Don't expect magic on Lesson 1, and don't expect it to go quickly. The most important skill of an academic coach is to set your expectations at a very, very low level. The official level of expectations for top academic coaches is zero.

Zero expectations are critical. As soon as you introduce the concept of correct or incorrect, as in I expect you to read this properly in the next 5 seconds, you are hampering learning and progress. This is easier said than done, especially when your child has read a word 6 times already and cannot even recognize the word 3 days later.

Some children will step through each letter in Lesson 1 saying the letter sounds in order, and showing no recognition that the letters are grouped into words. We spent at least 3 weeks on the first lesson and moved on to Lesson 2 even though I was having a hard time getting my child to say "CAT" instead of "C" – "A" – "T". Each time we practiced, I was perfectly comfortable with an abysmal performance and perfectly comfortable moving on to more advanced material before he mastered the prior material. By about Lesson 10, he could go back to the first few lessons and zoom through them. It turns out that this is a very common experience.

It wasn't until Lesson 20 when he could actually read words, sometimes the first time that he saw them, that I realized learning was taking place this whole time. When we got to the silent "e", the whole miserable process repeated itself, which is why silent "e" shows up in Lesson 26, and then it doesn't reappear until lesson 55. This timing won't work perfectly for each child, and the explanation for Lesson 26 explains how to address your specific needs in regard to silent "e".

Later, I put "THE" on the Word Board, and it stayed there for about 5 months. In our nightly reading, every time he would see "THE", he would try to sound it out, and I would remind him somewhat impatiently, that "THE" is a sight word, as it was on the previous page, and the 19 times before that this evening, and the 3,428 times before that as well. One day, he finally read "THE" properly, on the first try.

Again, during this somewhat frustrating time, learning was happening. All a parent can do is patiently present and explain the material, and wait for that developing skill set to decide that the time is right. In the meantime, take advantage of the fun hiding behind the occasional word. Once I learned this approach, everything else we did went more smoothly and much more quickly, without the tears. Learning is much more effective when you keep your expectations at the right level, which is Zero. It's not just your child who is learning.

Lesson 2

You can move on to Lesson 2 when your child can pronounce most of the words in Lesson 1, or two weeks have passed, whichever comes first. If you're not comfortable with the progress on Lesson 1, move to Lesson 2 anyway.

One of the hallmarks of a gifted parent-child team is to jump into advanced material before you're ready and sort out the mess. In the first part of the book, you should routinely go back to any lesson that your child is not comfortable with until she gets it right, and then you can draw a big X through the page.

To help with reading at this stage, invite your child to spell the words from each lesson. For each lesson, write the letter on half of an index card that you see in the lesson and put these cards in front of your child in random order. Read each word from the row. The first word will take a long time while your child finds all of the cards. The other words will go more quickly because usually only one card has to be replaced in the word.

For row one of Lesson 1, you will have cards for a, b, c, h, m, p, and t. The letter should be large, filling up most of the card. You ask your child to spell "at" and read it. After 3 minutes on a good day to 45 minutes on a really bad day, your child has "A" and "T" next to each other and reads the cards as "AT". Then you ask your child to spell "PAT" or "CAT".

The primary purpose of this exercise it to help your child master reading. The secondary purpose is for your child to see sound patterns, especially the "AT" that don't move from word to word and can just be pronounced "AT". This is what you want at some point, but do not help in any way, explain, give hints, demonstrate, or raise your eyebrows in hopeful expectation. The "learning" process consists of your child figuring something out on their own.

The spelling card exercise should wait until the last few sessions with each lesson. If you are spending two weeks on each session initially, do this exercise at the end of the 2nd week.

The spelling exercise is important for the basic sounds, and it is important for the silent "e" rule. We did this exercise for at least the first dozen or so lessons and only did it occasionally after that. We never did it for the more advanced phonemes. There's a time for the child to be able to spell words like "peal", "peel", "pie", etc., and that time can be as late as 2nd or 3rd grade. During earlier stages, the key goal is to open the child's mind to the richness of vocabulary.

Keep in mind that your child will have bad days caused by sickness, exhaustion, and hunger. You may not realize that your child is having a bad day until later. My rule of thumb for a 4 year old is that there are about two bad days in every five. If you are not making progress 2 out of 5 days, or your child completely forgets everything he learned on any given day, or your child is crying and whining the whole time, he is having a bad day. Do what you can on these days. I suggest either giving your child a single skittle for reading the words on each line, or picking a prior lesson and rereading it.

Lesson 3

Lesson 3 requires you to start using the Word Board, if you haven't done so already.

There are two primary uses of the Word Board at this stage. First, if your child is struggling with the "it" sound, put "it" and "bit" on the board. If your child has a hard time pronouncing "b", put "bit" and "bat" on the board.

The second and more important purpose of the Word Board is for vocabulary words. Lesson 3 has a bolded vocabulary word. Put "kin" on the Word Board. If you see a word that you think is very interesting, or your child doesn't know a word on any lesson, put it on the board. If you think my bolded selection is not interesting, don't put it up. I chose "kin" because it is a synonym for family, and synonyms are an important tool for cognitive skills, even more important than opposites, and I enjoy making up stories about our kin from the old country and sharing some of our imaginary family history.

I provided a definition of "tin" opposite Lesson 3, in case you want to use it on the Word Board. Not having a science background, nor finding anything in the house made of tin, I didn't use that word.

Once or twice a week, drag your child in front of the Word Board, and invite her to state a definition, act out, or indicate in some way that she knows the meaning of each word. Again, a child of four is not expected to recite the dictionary definition. If the word is "yuck", the child can stick out his tongue and make a face.

If the child can quickly read a word and gives a quick definition because they know a word, take it down. That word is going to go back up if they come across it in reading and the definition is forgotten. "Quickly" and "quick" are relative terms. Some children shout out a word and its definition instantly, and other children like to stare at a word for 3 minutes before talking.

Lesson 4

By this time, you might have some questions about the sentences below the list of words that your child is expected to read.

The primary purpose of the sentences in the first half of the book is to get your child to read individual words. I expect the child to read "Rat", "sat", "in", and "hat" and eventually read these like words, maybe someday on the first try. Reading comprehension will come at its own pace, even for a 4 word sentence. As the lessons progress, the sentences become a bit more challenging in the word choice and concepts.

The sentences are an independent exercise from the words, subject to the constraint that the words in the sentences usually appear in the current or prior lesson. Reading an entire sentence is a parallel learning process to reading individual words, and in this book the two processes move at different speeds. As the book progresses, some of the sentences introduce a bit of thinking.

The differences between phonics for early Pre K and phonics for Kindergarten is that an older child can hold a pencil, write letters, and learns at a faster pace. Older children are more comfortable with sentences. That is why this workbook is organized around lots of words, fewer sentences, much discussion, and no writing.

For advanced vocabulary, it's not important that your child knows that a vat is a tub in a ketchup factory that they use to mix the ketchup before bottling, although there's a great video on the internet from the Discovery Channel that's worth watching, and I encourage you to take advantage of the internet as needed to help define words. What is important is that your child just found out that tub has a different name if it is located in a different location or has a different purpose, and if she doesn't get it yet, she's thinking about it. Your child is on the verge of a thinking explosion, and these words are going to set the stage.

I include in the commentary aspects of the vocabulary that might spur your interest in a particular word in the hopes that if your enthusiasm for words grows, you will share it with your child and have a bit more fun with phonics.

The primary emphasis of this phonics course is thinking. For a gifted child, which I define as a child who has a parent determined to have their child go through most of the lessons in this book, learning to read is a foregone conclusion. With thorough coverage of phonics, strong reading is inevitable. Our goal is that by the time your child can read, she'll also have a much larger vocabulary, full of words with conceptual content and cognitive load, and be a much stronger thinker.

Lesson 5

The vocabulary words in Lesson 5 demonstrate where this book is heading.

Rap and lap require a bit of fun with the lesson. As the words become more interesting, feel free to spend more time talking about words and less time reading them. "Rap" is revisited in the commentary in Lesson 47, where the difference between rap, thump, knock, bang, and crack are discussed. By the end of the book words are presented with like or different concepts and not phonetically. For the purposes of Lesson 5, it's enough to introduce rap on its own.

Please act out these words, and invite your child to demonstrate them. Even if you're not much of a singer, try to make a song from some of the words. If a word suggests a messy experiment in the kitchen, have a messy experiment.

Lesson 6

The average child is going to struggle with the first 5 lessons if this is his introduction to reading and if he started the course early. If this is the case, do the first 5 lessons again before moving on.

Lesson 8

The word "kid" suggests a discussion of other names for baby animals. There are dozens of fun and obscure names for baby animals. Later, after your child has covered most of the letter and cluster sounds, feel free to post 20 of these on the Word Board and quiz your child at the Word Board a couple of times a week.

In the Test Prep Math series for 2nd through 4th grade, my coaching advice includes a strong prohibition against telling your child anything or helping in any way. I have defined a GAT Parenting Skill called Learning or Telling, and the general rule is not to tell anything. I'm fighting a culture of Spoon Feeding. A reader asked how I apply this to reading. I ask a lot of questions in reading and wait for answers, but during the reading process I generally tell most of the time in the attempt to pack my child's brain with as much information that will fit, and then pack a bit more on top of that. When we read together, if I see a new vocabulary word, we might spend five minutes on it. There are some instances in this phonics course where the child can figure out something for themselves, and I'm willing to endure 20 minutes of a blank, silent stare for an attempt at an answer, followed by 3 wrong answers and 6 random guesses. During most of the course, however, I'm usually doing a lot more talking.

Lesson 9

At some point in the first quarter of the book, your child will be comfortable with pronouncing the 20 consonant letters. The next step is becoming comfortable with the "ig" and "ill" sounds as a cluster. Once your child transitions from "I" – "G" to "IG", the pace of each lesson will increase.

I expect the pace for most children will still be very slow at this point, perhaps 2 weeks per lesson. There are 100 lessons in this book, and ideally you get through it in a year. The pace starts out slowly and speeds up on its own. There are some lessons later in the book that might be completed in one sitting.

Lesson 11

Before starting Lesson 11, reread Lessons 1 through 10. If your child reads a page quickly, cross it off. Incorporate review as a weekly or every other week event.

Lesson 14

This lesson introduces the first 2 sight words, "and" and "the". The sight words are usually on the last line of each lesson starting in Lesson 18, and each sight word should go onto the Word Board for as long as it takes until the child can read it.

Since "the" is completely unrelated to phonics, it is included here to give your child a head start. As I mentioned in the introduction, it stayed on our Word Board for many months. The Word Board should get very full.

Lesson 21

You may notice that some parent commentary opposite each lesson sounds like a discussion. A typical lesson might consist of 5 minutes of actual sounding out words, 10 minutes of complaining, whining, or rolling on the floor, and 10 minutes of exploring the vocabulary in front of you. I add questions, ideas, stories, explanations and hints.

The definition I provide for the word "lot" can spur imagination and show a child things she's never seen before. I don't expect every child to be enthralled by the word "lot", but there are over 2,000 words in this course to work with. The discussion starts the process.

Lesson 26

This lesson introduces the silent "e". If your child was making progress and getting the hang of phonics, let me remind you to reset your expectations at the proper level, which is Zero. The silent "e" is not part of a steady progression, but a leap, and it may take the child longer to make the leap. There are 3 silent "e" lessons, and then silent e reappears in Lesson 55.

At some point in the next few months, your child will get the hang of silent "e". It is hard to predict how long this will take. You can invite your child to read words ending in "e" during your nightly reading.

If your child has no problem with the silent "e" in the next few lessons, then you can start alternating between lessons in this part of the book and the lessons that begin with Lesson 55. No workbook perfectly matches any child's progress. Before 2nd grade, I usually posted a list of page numbers for a workbook on the wall to track progress through different parts of the book simultaneously. If a page seemed impossible, we'd just skip it and come back to it when my child was ready.

Lesson 29 to 54

Lesson 29 marks the turning point in the book from basic phonics to advanced phonics. Lessons 29 through 54 cover consonant combinations and introduce vowel combinations.

Lesson 35 introduces "ay", as in day, and "ie" as in pie. You might consider a section on the Word Board for advanced consonant clusters and leave one example from each on the board for a long time, but not vowel clusters. I didn't put words like pie and day on the board. In my opinion, exercise of consonant clusters are more important than vowel clusters. In the next few years, vowel clusters will come naturally.

After Lesson 29, the emphasis shifts to conceptual vocabulary, including contextual use and shades of meaning, and these words might take more than a day to comprehend in depth even if your child can read the lesson quickly. Words should appear on the Word Board because they hold an interesting key to your child's cognitive development. If your child struggles with the pronunciation of "tomb" (Lesson 38) or "rolling" (Lesson 39), but they get through it with a little help, I don't recommend putting it on the Word Board, unless you have a budding archeologist enthralled with the concept of a tomb.

Words are important for different reasons. Some words are important to your child's ability to express herself and get through a book on her own with some understanding. I refer to this group as "vocabulary words". Other words introduce your child to the concept that there is a word for everything, words have shades of meaning and context, words convey concepts that have not been discovered before by the child, and these words spur imagination and induce thinking. I refer to the latter group as "conceptual vocabulary", and you can consider these words "brain building words".

Lesson 35 blandly states that the definition of the word "bust" is a statue of a person from the chest up and "burr" is a rough edge on metal. Lesson 35 also includes the definition for "spur". Some words on their own are good for imagination, like the word "fleck" which begs for a mental image. But for words like burr and bust, a bit more work is required. If burr is a rough edge on metal, find something made out of metal with a burr. If you can't find a burr, let your child read it for the phonetic value and don't put it on the Word Board. For words like "bust", a goofier definition is optimal. A bust is a statue that an artist made because he didn't have enough stone to make a whole body. Or maybe the subject was standing up to his chest in mud so the artist only made a statue of what he saw. Maybe it was a tar pit. For words like "spur", ask why a cowboy wears a spur. The answer is that the cowboy wants to hurry out of the pasture because a cow is wandering away and his horse is just standing there eating grass. The cowboy is yelling "yah" and the horse won't move. So the cowboy takes his sharp spikes and digs them into the sides of the horse, and the horse runs away so he won't get stabbed in the side again. When you are providing definitions, ask yourself what makes a word special, or why there is a special word at all.

Lesson 55 to 77

Lesson 55 reintroduces the silent "e", and then covers this concept and more challenging vowel clusters thoroughly. During Lessons 29 through 54, when things begin to go quickly, you can skip to Lesson 55, and alternate between this section of the book and the easier pages from Lessons 29 to 54 depending on whether your child is in a mood to work hard, or is having a bad day and needs something a bit easier to do.

By about Lesson 52 it should be obvious to you why this is a gifted phonics book and not just a regular phonics book. There are 4 different clusters on the 4 lines and a few miscellaneous clusters thrown in. Depending on where your child is in reading skills, or whether you started phonics early, late, or at the right time, this page will go quickly or take a long time. It doesn't matter. Your child is already on the way to advanced reading and it will happen at the proper time. The page will take a long time because our focus is the words and their definitions. There are 11 words that could motivate introductory research and science experiments. If you have a bunch of tools in the basement, you could introduce your child to the 1,000's of fasteners that exist and why they exist. You could try to make whey. You could get a candle and thoroughly cover sniff and whiff when you blow it out, or you could just have fun demonstrating the difference between nibble and gobble. This isn't so much a vocabulary exercises as introducing your child to many concepts that exist that most kids don't realize exist because they aren't introduced to them.

The Word Board should be part of the fun and not a chore. Your child will have learning chores later when he can handle them. In the meantime, if your child is fascinated with scar and scab, put them on the Word Board with any other words in the vicinity that you think of. If scan goes on the Word Board, and you're child isn't thrilled with acting out scan and search and find, take it down.

Here's how gifted works. In Lesson 55, you see the word lobby, and explain it. When you are out and about, you point out a lobby to your child, and also point out foyer and vestibule and try to explain the defining characteristics and definitions. You are learning to be a gifted parent while your child is learning to be a gifted child. Porch also is in the ballpark, but it's outside, not inside. Once we walked to the library and ran up to each building on the way to see if it had a lobby or a foyer or vestibule. The three words lobby, vestibule, and foyer are not useful in everyday conversation to a 4 year old. The ability to evaluate and characterize his world is absolutely vital.

Lesson 78 to 93

This lesson begins introducing conceptual math vocabulary, as well as more challenging sight words, and the last of the vowel and consonant clusters.

At this stage in the book, you can be more choosy which vocabulary words you and your child want to put on the Word Board, and which ones you read once and never revisit again. You may have fun with turn, spin, roll, and twirl from Lesson 91, or hold, grasp, clutch, and clasp from Lesson 89. It may seem like a stretch that your child could get through these words if you are struggling through Lesson 1, but this is months away, and phonics will work its magic in that time.

Lesson 85 lists the number words up to twelve, and Lesson 87 introduces ordinal words up to twelfth. Your child will start working with these words soon thereafter, so if she can read them once, you can spend the rest of the time using the words.

In addition to cognitive skills tests, some school districts also give a child a standardized test to gauge academic skills. If your school district uses a standardized test, then some of the number and ordinal words can go on the Word Board.

We put all of the sight words on the board and they stayed there for a very long time. In retrospect, the conceptual vocabulary words had a much bigger payoff, and the sight words came along at their own pace.

Lessons with conceptual math vocabulary are very important and should be explored thoroughly. For example, Lesson 83 has words like "long", "higher", and "widest". Lesson 88 covers "between", "right", "above" and similar words. Lesson

19

93 defines shapes. If your child is going to sit for a cognitive skills exam, cover the math vocabulary in this section of the book thoroughly at least 3 months before the test, regardless of your child's progress in reading, even if you have to do the reading. If a cognitive skills exam is not imminent, cover these pages very thoroughly when you get to them.

Lesson 95 to 101

These lessons include the first 6 vocabulary lessons for your child, as a precursor to what will come next in your child's At Home Schooling curriculum.

When I sorted through all letter combinations of 5 letters or less, I was surprised how many terms are dedicated to ships, and how accessible these terms are to children. Lesson 96 follows with the names of things under the ship.

Lessons 96 through 101 focus on synonyms and opposites at a fairly advanced level.

I would recommend posting every word from each lesson on the Word Board and inviting your child to define and describe what is interesting each word before taking it down. There are some words that are worthy of the Word Board that may be beyond the phonetic skills of your child. Rectangular prism is two of these words. Put them on the Word Board, and be prepared to read them each time.

We used the Word Board until about 2nd grade to help with vocabulary and advanced social studies or science terms. I didn't know how many terms there were for rocks until my son brought home a science test, and then all words for rocks went on the Word Board. Did you know that in some GAT programs, first graders have 3rd grade science books and 3rd grade grammar books? I did not know that. I did not know that 1st graders in this program all read at the 3rd grade level or higher, with at least one unfortunately exception. The Word Board saved us that year.

As soon I was enlightened by the science test, the hard way in my opinion, my three year old started phonics. On one Word Board, we had words like "Shale" and "Silt". Lacking room on the refrigerator, I bought a poster for the other Word Board and posted the first word, which was "CAT".

A few times a week, each child was dragged in front of the Word Board to see which words were mastered and which words would remain on the Word Board. If the child read "grim" with no trouble and made a tight lipped face, the word would come down. Some days, he might be laughing while trying to make a goofy expression. Other days he would be frowning and while trying to demonstrate "surprise" because the Word Board had accumulated 50 words.

A few years later, words rarely went on the Word Board, and if they did, they came down right away. Without realizing it, we were developing memorization skills to the point where new and advanced words with shades of meaning were memorized on sight. The Word Board played a vital role. Like a strong vocabulary, a strong memory is a powerful academic skill.

Phonics

Lesson 1

at   bat   cat   hat   mat   pat

an   ban   can   fan   man   pan

Man can pat cat.

Bat can fan man.

Lesson 2

had   mad   pad   pat   pan   had

at   sat   sad   man   mad   mat

Man had a can.

Cat sat at pan. Sad cat.

Kin means all of your relations. It can include your immediate family, but usually means family relations outside of the immediate family. Ask your child to list all of the family words she can think of.

Tin is a metal, and an element. Pewter is an alloy of tin which was used for plates in the Bronze Age. You are unlikely to have an example of tin in the house, but you might have something made of pewter.

Lesson 3

it   bit   fit   hit   lit   pit

in   fin   **kin**   pin   tin   win

Cat sat in a pit. Tin man sat in a pit.

Tin man pat cat. Cat pat tin man.

A vat is a large tub that holds liquid, typically found in factories that make food products.

Tin is also added to copper to form bronze. Bronze originally was formed by copper and arsenic, but the makers tended to die from arsenic poisoning so tin was substituted. Combining two metals makes for a stronger material. Tin was also used to make foil, but it was replaced by aluminum foil, which is still referred to as "tin foil" even though it doesn't contain tin.

Lesson 4

mat   rat   **vat**   hat   mat   cat

pan   ran   tan   van   **tin**   kin

Rat sat in hat. Hat sat in van.

Cat sat in van. Rat bit cat.

Rap is to knock quickly and lightly, stronger than a tap, and more impatient than a knock. Rap is also to sing in a very wordy and rhythmic way, with little regard for melody. If you make up short sentences with each word on a page, and say them quickly and rhythmically, you are rapping, as in "This is my rap it's about a map I'm going to tap that map in my rap do do do do do doot".

A lap is a complete tour of a designated course, as in "run a lap around the house", but also the thigh and hip area of a sitting person suitable for placing a book or a another person, as in "hold this book on your lap".

Sap is the blood of a tree, made of water and sugar. If you boil maple sap, you get maple syrup.

Lesson 5

cap   gap   **lap**   map   nap   **rap**

ran   rat   **sap**   sat   tap   tan

Rat ran lap in van. Cat ran lap in van.

Dan fit hat, pat, mat and cap in van.

Yet is best defined in a sentence, as in 'We haven't eaten dinner yet'. Yet is a very important word for kids with the correct learning attitude. If your child ever says "I can't do this", you should reply, "You can't do this **yet**."

Lesson 6

bet   get   jet   let   met   net

pet   pat   pan   vet   wet   **yet**

Cat in vat. Cat get wet.

Vet met cat. Vet pat cat.

Den is a house for bears, or a room in some houses that is supposed to be quiet, like a cave.

Lesson 7

Ben   ban   bat   bet   **den**   Dan

hen   men   ten   pen   pan   pat

Vet in pen.

Ten hens in pen.

Hens met vet.

A kid is a baby goat.   All baby animals and all groups of animals have a name.   A group of goats is called a tribe.

Feel free to skip bid or go into a long discussion.   A better word at this age is "offer", but bid is an offer with an expected reward, as in "I offer to let you skip your math workbook if you read this page 5 times without complaining", which is a bid that can accepted or rejected, as opposed to "I offer to clean my room because I'm in a good mood."

Lesson 8

bid　　bit　　bat　　ban　　den　　did

hid　　hat　　**kid**　　lid　　lit　　rid

Kid hid in pen.

Kid tap lid.

Ben let kid tap lid.

A gill is an organ that fish use to obtain oxygen from water, since they don't have lungs, and fish are surrounded by water.

A fig is a fruit.

Why did the pig hide a hat in the hill? Invite your child to make up a story about it. If he's totally surprised by this request, make up a goofy story and tell it to your child.

Lesson 9

big   dig   **fig**   pig   wig   is

dill   fill   **gill**   hill   pill   will

Pig can dig in hill.

Pig will dig in hill.

Pig hid hat in hill.

Toss is to throw the ball in the hopes that the person will catch it, as opposed to throwing the ball as hard and fast as you can. You can demonstrate both with a properly chosen soft ball or sock.

A loss is the opposite of a win, using the noun form of the verbs lost and won. Less is the opposite of more. You can just point to the rib cage, which is a cage, and is made up of ribs.

Moss is a small green plant that has no roots or flowers.

Fib is a lie, which is usually a bad thing, but fib is a lie in a context like a joke where the liar is not going to get into trouble. It's not a Word Board word because I'm reluctant to suggest concepts that might backfire.

Lesson 10

less   mess   yes   bib   fib   **rib**

loss   moss   **toss**   bib   best   has

Ben had a big mess.

Dan had less mess.

Demonstrate the difference between lob and toss.   When a ball is lobbed, it goes higher in the air than a toss. Both lob and toss are softer than a throw.

Sob and cry are similar but different, in that sob is crying harder and more loudly.

Lesson 11

Bob   job   **lob**   mob   rob   **sob**

bop   cop   hop   mop   pop   top

Bob had a lid.

Bob will toss it.

Ben will lob it.

Cog is a robot part that is round and has teeth. Cogs are found in other machines.

Bog is ground that is so wet and muddy that you would sink into it. If the bog is deep, a person could be turned into a mummy if they fall into it, like the Tollund Man.

Cot is a small fold up bed used for camping. What is the name for a bed that a baby sleeps in?

Lesson 12

bog　　**cog**　　fog　　hog　　jog　　log

bog　　Bob　　bop　　top　　cot　　cat

A bog is wet.

A log is in a bog.

A hog is a pig.

A pig has ribs.

A pun is a joke that uses two meanings of the same word. Why are fish so smart? Because they swim in schools.

Tut is of course a nickname for king Tutankhamun.

Lesson 13

bun   fun   pun   run   sun   fun

cut   gut   hut   mutt   nut   Tut

Mutt is in hut.

Tut met mutt in hut.

Tut cut log.

Sum is the total when two numbers are added together. 4 is the sum of 2 plus 2. What is the sum of 3 + 3?

How are jug, bottle, mug, and cup similar and different? You may have to show your child a picture of a jug and compare it to a mug. In addition to being bigger than a mug, a jug also has a rounded neck that you can stick a cork in. Mug is usually bigger than a cup, and jug is usually bigger than a bottle.

Lesson 15

back   Jack   lack   **pack**   quack   rack

tack   yack   yuck   **sack**   sun   sat

Jack has a pack.   Bob has a sack.

Jack put sack in pack

A beck is a mountain stream.   Why not just call it a mountain stream? Because there is a special name for just about everything.

A tick is both the sound of a watch or clock, and a blood sucking vampire creature in the spider family. Feel free to do an internet research project on ticks, spiders, and insects.

Yuck is a word from the next lesson.

Lesson 16

beck   deck   neck   peck   kick   lick

Nick   pick   quick   Rick   sick   **tick**

A tick bit Nick.

Yuck.

Nick is sick.

While a demonstration of the word "mock" may spur the imagination of your child, it could also backfire when they practice this new concept. It did for me.

Jock is a slang term for a high school student who is involved in sports all year long.

Buck is a male deer.

Lesson 17

dock   lock   mock   rock   sock   sack

buck   duck   luck   muck   tuck   yuck

The bog has muck.

The sock is in the muck.

This isn't a good time to teach contractions, which might be tricky, but it's a good time to see if your child notices the apostrophe. Later in the book all sight contractions are presented.

A bunt is a small hit. A dent is best demonstrated with clay or an aluminum can.

Lesson 18

all   call   fall   hall   tall   wall

ball   bell   fell   tell   well   yell

can't   **dent**   hunt   hint   want   went

The ball has a dent.

Get the ball.

"The" is a very important sight word. It takes some children 3 months to properly read "the" in a book when they are beginning readers because they are sounding out words. This word may be on the Word Board for many months, and for many months your child may be unable to read it because she is trying to sound it out each time.

Bull is a male cow, and also the name of the male for many other animals, like a seal or a shark.

Ping will be defined in Lesson 39.

Lesson 19

ball   bell   Bill   bull   fall   fell

full   hall   hill   best   nest   rest

king   ping   ring   sing   wing   of

The bell rings in the hall.

The bull fell on the bell.

"Haw" is an old word for laugh, as in "hee-haw". It is also an exclamation of incredulity and the fruit of the hawthorn tree. I'm usually just stick with hee-haw, which is fun to say if said with a drawl.

Wand is a tool of magicians and wizards and a great word to introduce the concept of words that don't sound like they are spelled.

Raw is uncooked (meat) or not ready to eat (fruit).

Lesson 24

bed   fed   led   med   red   wed

big   dig   fig   pig   wig   zig

dig   dipping   mop   mopping   **sip**   sipping

The pig is in the pot.

The pig is red.

A sill is the shelf on a window. The piece of wood underneath the sill, inside the house, is called an apron. Cod is a large fish that ends up in fish sandwiches. Pow is an onomatopoeia used in comic books.

Mod is short for modern (and module).

Bow with a short O is the front of a ship or a bend at the waist in the face of applause. Bow with a long O is a ribbon tied in a knot. It may confuse your child to introduce alternate sounds of the ow cluster this early in the book. Becoming comfortable with confusion is an important academic skill for both children and their academic coaches.

Lesson 25

cod   mod   nod   pod   rod   sod

bow   cow   how   now   pow   wow

hit   hitting   sit   sitting   **sill**   silly

The big pig is sitting on a log in a bog.

Shin is the front of the lower part of the leg.

Tote is to carry a big bag, which it turns out is called a tote as well.

Mane is the hair on the neck. Two popular animals have hair on their neck.

Lesson 26

at   ate   mad   made   man   **mane**

fin   fine   pin   pine   **shin**   shine

tot   **tote**   rob   robe   cod   code

A tote is a big bag.

A _____ has a fin.

A _____ has a mane.

App is a small computer program for phones.   If your child skips over this without asking what it means don't bring it up.

Lob is to toss the ball, and lobe is the bottom part of the ear. As a reminder, lob is a toss that goes higher.

Glob is a handful of something that oozes or is moist like mud or slime. Marbles can't be a glob.

Lesson 27

tap	tape	hat	hate	app	ape

dim	dime	bit	bite	hid	hide

hop	hope	**glob**	globe	**lob**	**lobe**

Lob the ball at the wall. Toss the ball.

Pick up the ball.

A rune is a letter in ancient writing. It's so old, no one knows what it sounds like or what it means.

A dud is a firecracker that fails to explode when it's lit. Dude is a nickname that cowboys use to describe people who don't know how to ride horses. Dude is also what 2nd grade boys call each other, as in "Hey bro man dude!"

A kit is a group of things used to make something or do something, like a science kit, a cooking kit, a makeup kit or an overnight bathroom kit.

Lesson 28

can	cane	cap	cape	tap	tape

Tim	time	**kit**	kite	win	wine

dud	dude	cub	cube	run	**rune**

Tim tapped the cane.

Is a box a cube? A box is a cube.

Hup is a term used in the army when marching that has been mispronounced for so long that no one knows what word it originally was.

Gus is a nickname for August, Gustav, and other names. Many short names are nicknames for longer names.

Words that are sounds have a special name worth bringing up. The word is onomatopoeia.

Lesson 31

dim	him	Jim	Kim	**rim**	run

dip	hip	lip	rip	sip	tip

ash	**dash**	lash	**sash**	wash	trash

sun	fish	sunfish	pat	leg	bus

Jim takes a sip of from the rim.

The rim is on the top of the cup.

The sash is up.

Vex is to annoy someone on trivial matters. You can work this into conversation instead of the word annoy.

Fizz is the sound soda makes

Biz is short for business in the movie and theater industries. Like using the term "med" for medication, "biz" is trying to make a word sound good when the speaker dislikes the concept.

Rex is the nickname of a big dinosaur with a lot of teeth.

Potty is the small bowl or product that looks like a toilet, used by small children as a toilet, but it has no plumbing and is not a toilet.

Lesson 35

day   hay   may   ray   say   way

lie   pie   tie   day   dig   dog

burr   fur   purr   blur   **spur**   **slur**

bust   dust   just   must   **rust**   key

The pet has fur and can purr.

The pet is not a dog.

The pet is a _____ .

Soy is a protein from soybeans that ends up in lots of products. Do a research product in your cupboard or pantry to find out what has soy in it.

Coy is not talking when you are shy or in trouble.

How many of the syllables in each compound word have to do with the word's meaning? Hotdog, catfish, and mailbox have 0, 1, and 2. Invite your child to think about each compound word when you encounter them in regular reading.

Lesson 36

doe   hoe   Joe   boy   coy   joy

soy   toy   toe   tie   torn   tea

out   hour   pour   **sour**   flour   scout

pour   pouring   scout   scouting   purr   purring

hot   dog   hotdog   cat   fish   catfish

Bob pours soy in the tea.

The catfish will not purr.

Dew is the water on grass in the spring and fall when the night is cold and the day is warm. If your child responds with "why", it's because air holds water, and air holds more water when it's hot than when it's cold.

Haul is to pull or drag something very heavy, with purpose. Lug is very similar, but with less enthusiasm.

When you are going to define "author" to your child, get a favorite book that also lists the illustrator and discuss both concepts. Show the publisher's name and describe what a publisher does.

Lesson 37

dew   **few**   hew   mew   new   many

gem   hem   limb   kiss   miss   sister

auto   **haul**   maul   haunt   **author**   vault

bath   path   math   with   cow   cowboy

A few cowboys ate many hotdogs.

The cowboys led the cows on the path.

This Lesson introduces the "long O sound for no apparent reason" and the silent B. As you can see, silent B can make an O long or make it sound like a U.

Ton is a word for 2,000 pounds (in some countries including mine) when you talk about the weight of really big things.

When an arm is numb, it has no feeling. You can demonstrate by asking your child to close her eyes and tell her you are touching her arm but don't. That is what she would feel if her arm is numb.

Jamb is the board that runs up the side of a window. There is one on each side and they sit on the sill. Doors also have jambs.

Lesson 43

stew   stick   **stiff**   still   stir   stock

flag   **flaw**   flap   flat   **fleck**   fled

brag   bran   bred   brick   bring   Brit

other   another   brother   sister   walk   talk

The other brother fled the shed.

The sister put stock in the stew.

Stub is either the end of a pencil after the rest has been worn away, or to hurt your toe when you trip on something.

Stud is a 2-by-4 in the wall that the wall boards are nailed to.

Stun is to shock someone so that they're frozen. Please act out the difference between surprise, shock, and stun.

Stow is to put something away neatly in the place where it goes.

Bloom is the part of flower growth when the flower opens. You can draw a flower growing in stages and then get to the bloom stage at the end. The first stage where the flower goes from seed to little plant is when it sprouts, which is a vocabulary word in the second half of the book.

Lesson 44

stub   stop   **stow**   stuck   **stud**   **stun**

scrap   screw   scrub   throb   throw   threw

boom   doom   room   zoom   **bloom**   broom

bath   room   bathroom   bedroom   bathtub   mushroom

Ben scrubs the tub in the bathroom.

Ken stows the flag in the box.

111

Chapped lips are dry and cracked. Lips chap in cold weather or in the sun.

Span is the distance between two things, like your fingers when you hold your arms out. Glum is kind of sad in general, not necessarily about a specific thing.

Glib is being goofy when you should be serious.

Glut is the too much when you have too much of something.

Shaft is the pole of a spear or shovel. But it's also the opposite - a tunnel for a cave or elevator. How cool is that?

Spew is a fast, strong flow of something liquidly.

chap   chalk   chat   chess   chew   chin

span   sped   spell   spew   spin   spit

glib   glob   gloss   glow   **glum**   **glut**

raft   after   **shaft**   draft   craft   crafty

There is a glut of floss in the bathroom.

The carpet spans the room.

Chip is both to cut a small bit of something, and the bit itself.

Chum is both a big bucket of fish parts to feed a shark, or your friend, or if you're sick of your friend, both.

Spur is a spiky wheel on a cowboy's boot to poke horses to make them move which was first introduced in Lesson 35. It is also a verb to get someone to do something quickly, usually in a good way, without stabbing them with pointy wheels.

Spar is to practice fighting.

Speck is a tiny piece of something like dirt on a table It is similar to fleck.

Bay is a small body of water with the sea on one side and land on the other sides. This is a loose definition.

Spud is a nickname for a potato.

In case you were wondering, Ben is a ship.

Lesson 46

chick   check   chill   chip   chop   **chum**

spot   spun   **spur**   **spar**   **speck**   spud

bring   cling   ring   sing   sting   wing

bay   clay   day   say   stay   way

Ben's chum has spurs. Ben's chum is a _____.

Ben has a rudder. Ben is a _____.

Drab is a boring, slightly dark color.

Thud is a low noise when you drop a book on the floor. It's not as loud as a bang or a crack, but stronger than a thump. It also means to make noise, like bang on a door, which is louder than both knocking and rapping.

There aren't enough "augh" words for a whole line, and laugh is a sight word, so laugh goes on the Word Board.

Lesson 47

drab   drag   draw   **drift**   drill   drip

thin   thumb   thud   thick   thing   thank

batting   beeping   cooking   digging   ending   falling

laugh   laughter   laughing   catch   catching   caught

I am a cook. I am cooking stew.
The stew looks drab.

Stand a book up on the table and demonstrate the opposite of swat and hit.

Swab is a cloth or bad used to clean something, and it's also the cleaning.

Droll is a word for "funny" from about 100 years ago.

When you make a goal, plan is the list of steps you also make to get there, and the act of making the steps. Give your child the goal of cleaning a room, and ask for the plan. A plan for a craft would be more fun.

Plow is the set of big blades pulled by a tractor that makes furrows in the soil to put seeds in. It's also the big shovel on the front of trucks to push earth or snow. It's also the act of turning up the earth with a plow to make room for seeds, as opposed to the tool.

Lesson 48

swab　　swing　　swan　　**swat**　　**sway**　　swell

droll　　drop　　drug　　drum　　draw　　drab

plan　　plod　　plug　　plus　　play　　**plow**

cough　　dough　　ought　　rough　　enough　　thought

Get the book.

Swat it, sway it, drum it, and swing it.

Thaw requires a science experiment with a glass filled about an inch with water, which then goes into the freezer to freeze, and out to thaw, repeat many times.

Swap means to trade something. It is pronounced "swop". Grub is baby insect.

You can grin at any time, but you can only smile when you're happy. Otherwise, a grin and a smile look the same. The problem with little kids is that they tend to feel happy as soon as they grin, so I differentiate a grin from a smile by degree – grin is less, and smile is more.

For grim, make tight lips, and differentiate it from a smile. For grit, make the grim look and show your teeth a little. Ask your child to grin and look grim without smiling.

Sneer is almost the same as grit, but you only how the top teeth. Of course, these facial expressions are used for different reasons.

Lesson 51

cross   crow   **crud**   crumb   crew   crick

snip   snub   snuck   snug   snow   show

straw   **strap**   strip   stripe   string   strut

angle   apple   bubble   buckle   candle   fiddle

Jim washes the crud off the prow of the ship.

A strap with a buckle is a belt.

Whiff is a smell that's only there faintly or momentarily. Sniff is how your nose looks for it.

Smug is being too proud about your awesomeness.

Tell your child to leave the room. Hide something small so that it's visible but hard to spot. Have your child look for it from one spot in the room without moving. She's scanning.

Which two words in the last line are opposites? Demonstrate them.

Lesson 52

whack   what   whey   wick   **whiff**   sniff

smack   small   smell   smock   smog   smug

scab   **scan**   scar   scat   skid   screw

giggle   gobble   handle   kettle   middle   nibble

Smell a whiff with a small sniff.

The cat scans the room for smog, then scats.

Whit is a tiny amount.

Trek is a small, adventuresome trip.

Trim is to cut a small part around the outside of something.

Writ is something in writing, usually official. If you are eyeing law school, put it on the Word Board and find something in the mail that is close enough like your credit card terms and conditions. If you are not eyeing law school, don't put writ on the Word Board; it's only on the page to fill out the line with the "wr" sound.

Lesson 53

whip   whit   who   what   why   where

track   tray   **trek**   trick   **trim**   trip

wrap   wreck   wren   wrist   wrong   writ

noodle   paddle   pebble   pickle   poodle   puddle

The noodle paddles on a raft in the stew.

The wren eats the noodle.

Knack is a special ability, like a knack for reading.

Knoll is a small hill, and knap is the top of a small hill. Ruffle is when a bird shakes their feathers or when someone messes up your hair. Knick is out of use and it's definition unreliable, but I needed another kn word.

Take away the k, and you've got a different word, but sometimes a word that is out of use or slang. Here's what you get when you take away the k: nap is a short sleep, nick is what you get when you chip a chip off of something, nob is an old word for head, nock is the slot that an arrow head goes in at the end of an arrow shaft, noll is an old word for the top of the head.

Lesson 54

troll   trot   truck   is   it   its

knack   knap   knick   knob   knock   **knoll**

knoll   knit   knot   know   gnaw   gnat

puzzle   rattle   **ruffle**   **rotten**   sample   staple

cup   cupcake   by   to   into   too

A troll has a knack for tricks.

The troll is rotten.

Abba is an old word for father.

Jade is the name of a green stone, and the name of a color that looks like the green stone.

For "mate", I'm going with the pirate definition, as in "Ahoy there mate!"

Paddy is a wet field where rice is grown. What do muddy and paddy have in common?

Wade is to walk through a deep puddle carefully, as opposed to jump in it.

Discover the differences between foyer, lobby, and vestibule. We decided that foyer is part of the entry way where you wait, vestibule is a bit bigger, has more art, and more routes into the building (like 3), and a lobby has a desk, a guard, and elevators nearby.

Lesson 55

abba   Bobby   hobby   gabby   **lobby**   babble

add   odd   buddy   daddy   muddy   **paddy**

at   ate   date   gate   late   mate

add   mad   made   fade   **wade**   **jade**

it   ite   bite   kite   white   write

Bobby has many trucks. Bobby plays with trucks.

It is his hobby.

Tote is to carry something big called a tote.

Ask your child which 3 words on this list are not words at all, if you haven't already done so.

Fluke is a flat worm, and a fun word to say.

Rude is anything you do at the dinner table besides eat and pleasantly talk about your day.

There are 3 words on this page that aren't words.

Lesson 56

egg	buggy	foggy	piggy	bigger	juggle
ot	ote	**tote**	vote	quote	wrote
dud	dude	rude	uke	duke	fluke
boo	moo	zoo	boot	food	hoop
us	as	be	for	my	not

The other brother fled the shed.

The sister put stock in the stew.

Apollo is the name of a Greek god and a type of rocket used to go to the moon. Both of these are worth exploring with research projects.

Rage is anger that is angrier than regular anger, which you both can act out, along with fury, irritation, and tantrum. Or you can just ignore rage and stay positive.

Vibe is nickname for the vibraphone. Search for videos on the Louisville Leopards to see the vibe in action.

Lobe is the bottom of the ear. It's also a roundish part of something. What do globe and lobe have in common?

Lesson 57

| ill | belly | dolly | hello | holly | **Apollo** |

| babe | safe | cage | page | rage | wage |

| **vibe** | tribe | scribe | hide | ride | tide |

| **lobe** | robe | globe | code | rode | joke |

| found | hound | mound | pound | round | sound |

The hound walked around the round mound.

The Apollo ship went to the moon.

The belly of the a ship is a hull.

Glide is to fly with no engine or without moving the wings (as in a bird).

The silent K is using its super power again. Nife is the earth's core, but knife is a cutting tool.

Loon is a bird similar to a duck.

There's only one good way to define yoke, and it involves a tiny hand, a bowl, and a wasted egg. Otherwise, yolk doesn't really belong on that line. It was originally yoke, but yoke is less exciting than cracking an egg.

Find a piece of string or shoe lace and demonstrate a loop. It's a circular shape with a crossing point.

Broke is the past of break.

Lesson 58

bake	cake	fake	lake	make	rake
wide	**glide**	pride	slide	wife	knife
poke	woke	**yolk**	broke	choke	smoke
hoot	loon	**loop**	noon	poof	roof
door	pour	order	actor	color	floor

The loon was baked into the cake.

The baker's wife got the knife. The loon ate the cake.

Spike is a sharp piece of metal used to hold the rail to the railroad tie. Look for an image of a railroad spike on the internet, because spike will just result in pictures of a guy named Spike.

Dike is a wall that keeps water out of a city when the residents decide to build their city right in the middle of an ocean or river. It is also called a levee.

Booth is a small tent at a fair where you can buy something. A file is a small tool for filing.

Gloomy is both dark (like the picture of a haunted house) and sad. Gloomy is more sad than glum. Glum is disappointed, but gloomy is hopeless.

hum   comma   jammy   summer   tummy   mummy

take   awake   brake   quake   shake   snake

bike   dike   hike   like   spike   file

scoop   soon   baboon   bloom   booth   gloomy

bike   biking   biked   fake   faked   faking

The quake makes the snake shake.

The loon is on the roof eating cake.

Make a funnel out of a piece of paper or paper plate and a stapler or tape.

Sole is the bottom of the foot and the bottom of a shoe. Tile is a rectangular piece of pottery on floors, walls, and roofs. Stroke is to pet sideways instead of up and down.

Shale is a type of rock. It will be a vocabulary word in elementary school.

Pale is a color that is very light. Use crayons to investigate this word.

Lesson 60

inn   bunny   funny   penny   **funnel**   tennis

spoke   **stroke**   hole   mole   pole   **sole**

pale   sale   whale   scale   stale   shale

mile   pile   **tile**   smile   while   dime

smile   smiled   smiling   hike   hiked   hiking

The baboon tells a joke.

The bunny smiles and the whale grins.

The mole is grim. The baboon's joke is not funny.

Guppy is a small fish that likes to eat mosquitos.

Cone is a math word. Make one out of paper and tape or staples, like the funnel from the prior lesson, and observe it in detail. How wide is the cone? How wide is it at the bottom, in the middle, at the top? The cone is a cylinder that can't decide how wide it wants to be. The funnel lacks a point.

Both sweatshirts and cars have hoods.

A wild animal that behaves and doesn't eat people is tame, like a cat, but not a lion in the wild.

Lesson 63

bass   cross   basset   fossil   glassy   blossom

cane   lane   **pane**   crane   plane   insane

dine   fine   line   mine   nine   pine

shone   stone   throne   hope   rope   **scope**

dine   dined   dining   shine   shined   shining

The basset hound sits on the
throne in the land of dogs.

Brook is a small creek, which is a small stream, which is a small river. You can run and jump over a creek, and probably just walk over a brook. Your legs will get wet wading across a stream, and you have to swim to get across a river or take a boat. Surprisingly, there is no word for a very large river like the Mississippi or Amazon. Ask your child to make one up.

Whoop is a loud cry of excitement. When you define whoop, you have to yell "whoop". Whoop should go on the Word Board just for fun.

better   bottle   bottom   kettle   letter   pretty

brook   crook   floor   shook   igloo   **whoop**

ape   cape   tape   drape   grape   shape

vine   shine   pine   swine   whine   pipe

egg   eggplant   eggshell   bed   time   bedtime

Does a bottle have more water than a kettle?

Does a creek have more water than a brook?

Bore is to drill into something. Core is the middle of a 3 dimensional shape, like the earth or an apple.   Does an orange have a core? This is a good word for imagination and thinking. Technically, stabbing an apple with a fork is not boring. You should use a pencil, but the word pencil contains a rule that is just beyond this book.

Foul means both unfair and really smelly. I would expect your child to act out smelly and foul while standing at the Word Board instead of repeating the definition.

Brace is to strengthen by adding more material. Try to stand up a magazine or newspaper. Brace it with a few books.

Lesson 65

buzz   fizz   jazz   pizza   guzzle   puzzle

bore   **core**   more   sore   tore   chore

foul   four   hour   loud   mouse   noun

face   lace   race   **brace**   space   trace

race   car   racecar   no   on   or

Bore into the core of an apple with a fork.

Can you guzzle pizza?

What is louder than a race?

Gripe is both to complain and the complaint. Swipe is a finger movement on touch screens and a hand movement in cleaning. It is both "to swipe" and "a swipe".

Bound is like bouncing and walking at the same time.

Stare is to look for a long time, and glare is to look angrily. Ask your child to demonstrate the difference between stare and glare without smiling or laughing.

When fruit grows on a tree, it is very hard at first, and then it gets softer and tastier over the next few weeks. Growers usually pick fruit 2 weeks before it is ripe so that by the time it is in your kitchen, it is just about ripe.

Lesson 66

bare	care	**glare**	**stare**	scare	share
ripe	wipe	gripe	**swipe**	tire	wire
shore	snore	store	hose	nose	rose
about	aloud	**bound**	cloud	could	doubt
mayor	motor	razor	cursor	doctor	flavor

The man with the cape glared at the mayor.

The mayor snores.

Shire is the country where hobbits live and a really big horse.

A guise is your theme for your disguise. It used to be the opposite of disguise but not anymore.

A luge is an toboggan used at the Winter Olympics. Does your child remember what a mound and a knoll are? A wildlife refuge is a park for animals to protect them from hunting and development.

Wise is old and smart, as opposed to just smart. Smart is to know a lot of things and have the skills and patience to think through challenging problems. Wise is not only smart, but to have way more knowledge of things based on experience, which is why wise usually requires old.

Lesson 67

base   case   vase   chase   **crate**   plate

Shire   rise   **wise**   **arise**   **guise**   bite

chose   close   those   huge   luge   **refuge**

flour   found   hound   house   **mound**   mouth

harbor   indoor   backdoor   outdoor   mirror   sailor

A huge house is called a manor.

The sailor lugs the crate from the harbor to the ship.

Fume is a smelly or poisonous gas, and plume is a big featherlike thing, possibly a feather, possibly a fume of smoke. Yule is an old word for Christmas.

Bail is to remove water from a boat with a bucket because the boat has a hole in it and is sinking.

Loony means crazy, usually visibly, so you have to act it out.

Dune is a hill made out of sand that is long but not necessarily tall. It is made by the wind blowing sand into a pile.

Mule is an animal that is half horse and half donkey, used to carry a heavy load.

The first 3 lines have letter combinations with 2 different sounds.   When your child reads these lines, he will be experiencing a process that is explicitly measured by cognitive tests. If your child read "have" with a long a, and it didn't sound right, so your child tried again with a different sound, you just witnessed the process. If your child said "have" with a long a and then you both laughed, then you have the core skill required for this process, which is to address mistakes with a lack of frustration and a lack of anxiety.

Lesson 70

mayor   motor   razor   cursor   doctor   flavor

blew   chew   crew   drew   flew   knew

view   heal   meal   peal   real   cereal

cheese   please   ease   unease   **cease**   **crease**

paste   taste   waste   coast   **roast**   toast

The mayor ate a meal of cheese and cereal.

The mayor chewed the cereal.

The cereal tasted like paste.

The third best definition of north is where the north pole is. The second best definition is to look at globe. The best definition of all is to point when you're inside, and then to point later when you are a few blocks from your house. The difference between these three definitions is the level of cognitive skills that are required. North should go on the Word Board with south, west, and east. By the way, the words are capitalized only when they refer to the location, as in the North, and not the direction.

Lesson 71

fort   **sort**   forth   **north**   short   sport

end   finish   cease   quit   stop   close

begin   start   **dawn**   rise   sprout   spring

increase   **decrease**   just   list   try   was

Draw a small map of your house.

Sort your toys by color.

Add your toys to the map.

Chive is a plant related to an onion whose leaves are used as ingredients in cooking. Thrive is to increase or improve in a healthy way.

Thrive is an advanced word but I was running out of "ize" words. Thrive means to get better at reading because you have a parent that fosters reading and education.

Lune is a 17th century math word. Draw 2 circles that intersect by about 80%. The lune is the crescent shape. Lune is not a math word, but it's just a cool concept.

Pure requires a science experiment, starting with "pure" water, and then add sand. Poor it through a paper towel or coffee filter, and it comes out pure again, almost. Repeat.

Lesson 72

doze   froze   **cube**   tube   **lune**   **rune**

rune   tune   prune   lure   **pure**   sure

jail   laid   nail   pail   pain   rail

want   point   went   plant   front   parent

chive   five   drive   **thrive**   size   prize

Bob had a glass of milk.   It was pure milk.

Bob added prune juice to the milk.

Now the milk is not pure.

Chute is a slide with steep sides or is a tube.

A brute is someone who acts like an animal.

Fold a piece of paper in half, and then fold walls about an inch high on either side. Slide a penny down the chute. The difference between slide and chute is that a slide is for people and a chute is for luggage or other things.

"Vain" is an overly proud peacock, as opposed to vein, which is in your arm, or vane, which sits on top of the barn and measures wind direction. You can act out vain. I dropped vein and vane from the book because spelling rules might be 2 or 3 years away even for super gifted children. Nonetheless, I encourage you to cover these words anyway on your own.

Grief is horrible sadness because you lost your favorite stuffed animal or toy. Wail is a loud cry of grief. The difference between grief and sadness is that with grief, nothing can make you happy.

Pixie is a small fairy that doesn't fly, looks like an elf, and plays tricks on people.

Lesson 73

cute   lute   mute   brute   **chute**   flute

die   **brief**   chief   field   grief   **pixie**

rain   tail   vain   wail   braid   chain

air   fair   hair   pair   said   again

hair   cut   haircut   aircraft   airplane   airport

The airplane flew briefly.

The airplane landed on the empty field.

Drain is both the part of the sink where water goes, and the act of sending water through this part.

Waive and wave are homophones. They sound alike, but are spelled differently and mean different things. Do you see any homophones on the last line?

Keep in mind that at this stage, we're doing a thorough tour of vocabulary to set the stage for later stages.   I don't recommend using the flash card exercise to spell vowel clusters or homophones.

What is the difference between a coil and a loop? With string, a loop crosses once forming a single circle or ellipse, but a coil repeats.

Lesson 74

bee   eel   cheek   **deep**   peel   sleep

goal   goalie   eat   ear   bead   beak

drain   mail   plain   snail   **waive**   **wave**

boil   **coil**   coin   join   oil   oink

mail   box   mailbox   dear   male   peanut

Water is ice when cold and steam when hot.

What two animals on this list live in the water?

When you peel and apple, you get apple peels.

A ship starts with a keel. Ribs are added next.

ship

rib

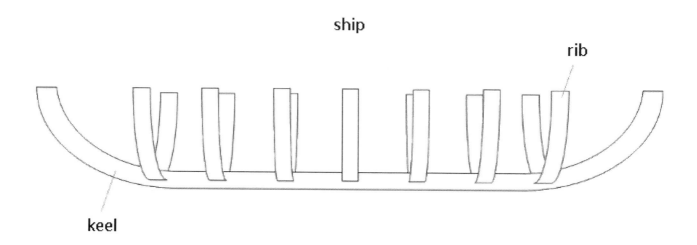

keel

A keel is the long board that spans the bottom of the hull. With wooden boats, the hull is built on top of it. It's not clear from research that airplanes have keels.

A beam is a long board that spans the ceiling on which the roof is built for older buildings. Beams can also be found under bridges. Unfortunately, the long beams under bridges are called stringers and the ribs are called beams, but it's still worthwhile to look up when travelling under bridges to point out the parts of the structure.

Toil is to work really hard for a long time. Void is a big expanse of empty space.

Joint is where two things meet. Sometimes they can move, sometimes they can't. A knee is a joint. The Greek word for knee is "gon". Look for joints on the body and on furniture.

Lesson 75

feed   feel   free   green   keel   knee

beam   bean   bear   each   east   fear

soil   **toil**   **void**   **joint**   doing   going

undo   unbox   uncle   under   until   unzip

mailbox   toolbox   jelly   jellybean   jellyfish   jellybeans

A table has a joint at the top of each leg.

The table joints do not move.

How many joints can you count on your body?

I count 15 just on the hand.

There are more homophones on this page, including heal/heel, leak/leek, dear/deer, hear/here. Hare is not a rabbit, but a cousin with longer legs and longer ears. Also, hares change their color to white in the winter.

Take a moment to appreciate the super power of "un". It makes a verb do the opposite of what it wants to do.

Peek means to look at something when you're hiding. It's a short look, as opposed to scan, which is a long, thorough look.

Heap is a big, messy pile.

Lesson 76

peek	reef	seek	teen	weed	agree

heal	**heap**	lead	leak	lean	leap

bear	dear	fear	hear	near	pear

unbend	unhook	unplug	untie	untuck	uncover

ate	eight	flour	flower	**hair**	**hare**

A white hare has white hair.

A black hare has black hair.

Look at the word hair.

Hair has one piece of hair under the dot.

Steer is what you do when you drive a car and you make it go in a different direction, but it is also a bull.

Shear is to cut the wool off of a sheep so that you can make wool yarn.

Peak is the pointy top of a mountain, sometimes covered with snow.

Weak is the opposite of strong, best demonstrated.

Appear is best demonstrated with a magic trick. Get a napkin and a coin, and do your best.

Lesson 77

queen   seed   speed   **steer**   teeth   weep

meal   mean   meat   near   **peak**   **weak**

rear   tear   wear   clear   **shear**   **appear**

dove   love   glove   oven   move   over

back   bow   hood   light   park   trip

The cowboy rides his horse over to the steer.

The steer appears to be asleep.   It's not.

If the steer could talk, it would say "Howdy".

Heave is to lift or pull something with effort. The "effort" is the difference between pull and heave. Shove is a push that is mad or mean.

Sigh breathing out slowly because of boredom or sadness. Gasp is to quickly breathe in from surprise. These words are the opposites in 3 ways: in/out, slow/fast, and bored/surprised.

Knead is to repeatedly mash bread or clay or pay dough until you can shape it into something.

Lesson 78

clean	cream	dream	**heave**	**knead**	need
sigh	thigh	eight	weigh	weight	height
high	higher	highest	big	bigger	biggest
above	cover	love	**shove**	over	push
was	**gasp**	were	when	which	who

Bill shoved the refrigerator.

His mom put up a sign that read "No shoving."

Bill tried to heave it. It was too big to heave.

Bill sighed.

Potion is a magical mixture that witches make in a cauldron. If you have food coloring, you can mix a potion in the kitchen, and also explore mixing two colors. Your child will likely want to repeat until all of the food coloring is gone.

Motion is moving, as in not stopping. Ask your child to demonstrate move and motion.

Might is strength and capability or possibility, as in "I might make you do another page if you don't pay attention" or "heave the refrigerator" with all of your might".

might   night   right   knight   alright   daylight

action   lotion   **motion**   **potion**   station   question

thin   thinner   thinnest   wide   wider   widest

short   shorter   shortest   tall   taller   tallest

of   off   once   open   our   we

Without talking, motion with your arms for someone to read these words. You can wave and point.

Move is shorter than motion. What does this mean?

What's the difference between sprout and grow? If a plant is tiny and grows quickly, it sprouts. Is there a similar word for sprinkle? Hand your child a salt shaker and a glass of water at the sink and ask again. You can pour a lot, or sprinkle a little.

Sprint is a quick run over a short distance, as fast as you can.

Lesson 80

height   fight   fright   light   neigh   sleigh

light   lighter   lightest   heavy   heavier   heaviest

bear   tear   pear   earth   earthquake   earthworm

spray   spring   sprang   **sprout**   **sprint**   **sprinkle**

are   ask   away   because   been   before

Run to the kitchen and sprinkle salt into the sink before your parent yells at you to come back and read.

This lesson is all math words.   Let you child build walls and towers with blocks, coins, books, or whatever you have handy that is stackable.   Let your child take as long as necessary to apply each word in this list to the various stacks and walls.   Books are useful for small and big, wide and narrow, short and long, but these words should be applied to the stacks and walls as well.

Please note that the words big and small are limiting both in early math and in high school writing, and it is my hope that you and your child drop them from usage. When you hear big or small, please correct your child by asking "Can you give me a better word than big (or small)?"

The questions below the words are the key to cognitive skills tests and writing good papers in high school.   Invite your child to draw each of the words.   If you ask the question, "What is the most important page in this book for my child's ability to master figure matrices on a cognitive skills test?", the answer is this page.

Lesson 81

long	longer	longest	short	shorter	shortest
tall	taller	tallest	short	shorter	shortest
small	smaller	smallest	big	bigger	biggest
high	higher	highest	low	lower	lowest
wide	wider	widest	narrow	narrower	narrowest

Demonstrate each word.

If something is wide, is it big?

If something is narrow, is it small?

I recommend that you use coins to work through the last line.   Combine is to make one pile out of two, and group is to organize the coins by denomination.   Separate is to move one coin or a group of coins from the other, possibly by denomination or count. Split is to do the same thing in your mind or with a pencil without moving the coins far away from each other.

Lesson 82

some   none   much   only   few   many

old   new   young   late   early   later

past   present   future   near   next   today

ideal   steal   wheel   feel   heal   kneel

together   apart   group   split   combine   separate

Explain each math word.

How are group and combine different?

How are near and "next to" different?

The first two lines plus through are sight words or sight words. All of these deserve to be posted. How long the words stay there varies by child.

Joint is back as a math word. Point to the knee and elbows as joints, then go around the house looking for more joints. Ask your child if he remembers that gon is the Greek work for knee, and if not, post it.

Agent is a secret agent. That's not a bad definition, but an agent is an agent because someone sends the agent. If the person just works on their own, then this person is a super hero or a detective who was not hired.

Thunk is a dull sound from dropping a book.

Lesson 85

belt   felt   knelt   melt   pelt   smelt

inside   outside   indoor   outdoor   horseshoe   headlight

so   she   does   do   done   don't

anybody   anything   anywhere   someone   something   somewhere

my   fly   him   his   her   hers

Look at a calendar.

Try to find the third day of the second week of the ninth month.

What day is it? Is it a Friday?

I don't expect a child to answer the questions about blocks without first spending time naming each place forwards and backwards. You can also do this exercise with coins, and you should do this exercise with words on a page, because sometimes cognitive skills tests don't have an obvious start to the line, but the tests are looking for strong readers, and strong readers know that the start of the line is always the left if no start is specified.

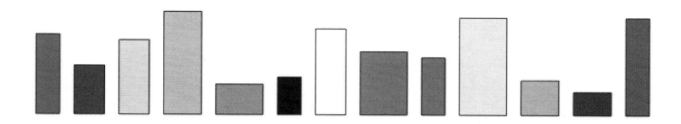

Which of these shapes is the tallest? The second tallest? Go through the list of ordinals.

Then repeat with shortest, widest, most narrow, lightest, and darkest.

It's not easy.   There are some ties in width, and the shading is hard to discern. If you want to build your child's visual perception, spend 20 minutes on this exercise each day for a week.

Which shapes are first and last? Since there is no door or kiosk in this picture, it is assumed that the head of the line is on the left.   But you can draw a door on either side if you want.

Lesson 86

first   tenth   third   fourth   eleventh   eighth

seventh   sixth   ninth   fifth   second   twelfth

second   minute   hour   day   week   month

year   half   quarter   time   calendar   clock

go   goes   he   had   has   here

Line up 13 blocks in front of the bathroom door.

The blocks have to go to the bathroom.

Which block is seventh in line?

Which block is third from the end?

How many months are in half of a year?

When I worked with my child on these concepts, I didn't just ask 3 questions on this page, I asked 36, just not in one sitting.

The last question demonstrates three or four advanced cognitive skills. Which word is in the middle? The middle of each row contains 2 words. What a goofy question. The answer could be beside or near, or both. There is only one question like this in this book. Test Prep Math for 2nd to 4th grade has many, many more questions like this.

Dread is how your child feels when it's time to do something unpleasant, like practice. I wanted to work this word in earlier, but I couldn't find a good place. Act out the difference between fear and dread.

Lesson 87

first   last   top   bottom   before   after

between   middle   above   below   right   left

close   closer   closest   far   farther   farthest

ahead   dread   behind   beside   near   next to

front   back   beginning   end   above   under

Which word in the list above is second from right and one down from the top?

Which word is to the right of the word in the bottom left?

Which word is in below the word in the middle?

For grasp, grab your child's forearm. For clutch, hug him from the side or hold something tightly in your hand. For clasp, find a clothespin and let it do the clasping.

Demonstrate is a good word to know but a hard word to read. I don't expect a child to pronounce this word properly, but I expect them to try a few times before the parent reads it and explains it if necessary. I could have just written "Act out", but this is offensive English and underestimates the child's verbal abilities. In the same way, if I wanted my child to add 2 and 3, I would say "Add two and three" or "what is the sum of two and three?". The first time, the child stares blankly, but after a demonstration and a little repetition, it's part of the vocabulary. I once saw the word "plus" used as a verb in a math book, and when I finished my tirade, my child was very clear on my expectations for his use of the English language while doing math.

Lesson 88

hold   **grasp**   **clutch**   clasp   **lug**   carry

pull   tug   drag   yank   pick   pluck

push   shove   before   after   early   late

soon   later   never   always   slow   fast

inside   outside   start   finish   within   center

What is the difference between grasp and clutch?

What is the difference between lug and carry?

Demonstrate these words.

Opposite is a fairly easy concept to introduce to an early three year old, and it's easy to catch up on opposites any time after that.   Children struggle with similarities and synonyms in the cognitive skills literature and on practice tests, which are a lot more complicated and require more advanced skills.

Lesson 89

pair   match   group   some   more   most

few   fewer   fewest   some   less   least

compare   same   alike   similar   different   equal

opposite   up   down   left   right   center

both   neither   find   most   least   none

Find a pair of shoes. Are they alike?

They are almost the same, but not equal.

What is the difference?

Turn and rotate are very similar, but rotate is usually associated with a specific destination, like upside down or half way. To twirl it, it has to be held up, and to roll it, it is usually on the ground. Spin is like turn but it goes more quickly and freely.

The cutting words are similar but all different. These can be demonstrated in a kitchen with an apple, except for rip. All of these except for chop can be demonstrated with paper.

Lesson 90

turn	**spin**	**roll**	**twirl**	wheel	**rotate**
cut	chop	trim	rip	split	separate
from	gave	help	little	upon	use
very	work	would	but	their	there
ease	please	breeze	peace	feast	least

Find a small plate.

Turn it. Spin it. Roll it. Rotate it.

What is the difference?

Vertical, horizontal, and diagonal are vocabulary words. This may seem like overkill, but diagonal is a very important concept. I never had luck with getting my children to memorize these words, but they knew the concepts.

Dawn is the time when the earth is viewable in the light of the sun, but the sun is not over the horizon yet. Twilight is in between dawn and sunrise, and is between the setting of the sun and darkness. After the sun sets behind the horizon, there is still light to see by, but it fades. You can explain this one evening. Evening is the period from around dinner time until bed time. After that, it's night.

Lesson 91

red   green   yellow   blue   black   white

orange   purple   pink   gray   brown   gold

light   lighter   lightest   dark   darker   darkest

bright   dim   dawn   **dusk**   sunny   cloudy

dark   light   pattern   **vertical**   **horizontal**   **diagonal**

Draw a square.   Inside the square, draw 3 lines.

Draw one vertical line, one horizontal line, and one diagonal line.

When is dusk?

What is the opposite of dusk?

Feel free to help with the reading as much as needed.   It's important for your child to think through these concepts. Your child will forget some of these words in a few weeks and not see them for a few years, and that's OK. We're learning how to see things.

A face is the side of a rectangular prism, which a rectangular version of a cube, but the sides of a rectangular prism are not equal. "How many words on this page have to do with a rectangular prism?" I could argue 11 do, but your answer may vary.

Rectangular prism is an important vocabulary word but perhaps out of grasp of an early reader to read it. Feel free to help with the reading. That is why the font of that last question is half parent half child.

Lesson 94

boat   ship   **helm**   cabin   deck   mast

paddle   canoe   sail   sailboat   rowboat   raft

bow   stern   port   starboard   prow   keel

oar   ocean   pirate   galley   star   ahoy

dock   pier   harbor   port   boatyard   wharf

The captain of the ship stood at the helm.

The captain of the rowboat grasped the oars.

Notice how the words in the top line one progress.

What is the difference between a seal and a sea lion? Among other things, sea lions walk on their flippers and seals scoot on their bellies.

There are at least three words on this list that might have nothing to do with water. Can you find them? Look for alternate meanings.

Lesson 95

brook   creek   stream   river   puddle   pool

ocean   fish   octopus   crab   seahorse   lobster

starfish   turtle   **seal**   **sea lion**   shrimp   squid

eel   wave   fin   gill   whale   school

The cartoon showed a seal walking on its flippers.

Seals don't walk on their flippers.

Seals scoot on their bellies.

Here are 24 common, knowable words.   Work out the differences with your child.   To start things off, a part is typically not the same as the rest of the whole, but could be, where a piece usually is, but not always.   A piece of cheese is different than a car part.   A missing piece of the puzzle is unique, but missing part can be found on the parts shelf with a dozen other identical parts.

The best way to approach these two words is with lots of examples and verbal experimentation.   I call that exercise pre-test prep.

Lesson 96

piece   part   bit   slice   half   some

whole   full   complete   entire   total   every

talk   tell   show   speak   say   chat

babble   mumble   sing   hum   gasp   **sigh**

The puzzle was missing a piece.

The car was missing a part, and the missing part was a wheel.

What is the difference between a piece and a part?

If you had a cookie, what is the difference between keep and save?

If you keep a cookie, it's in a box somewhere until it gets stale. If you save it, you are going to eat it later.

Or, if you save it, it's because a monster was going to eat it and the cookie was crying for help.

Lesson 97

keep	set	put	save	set	plop
get	buy	take	win	**earn**	pick up
silent	quiet	soft	low	still	hush
noisy	loud	cry	cheer	roar	yell

What is the quietest word on the fourth line?

What is the loudest word on the third line?

If you drop a penny in a class of water, what sound does it make? Is it ploop?

For the lines that begin with stop and right, brainstorm antonyms and shades of meaning. Enjoy thinking about these things without knowing them all right away or being 100% correct. It's more important to raise a thinker and not just a knower.

Lesson 98

stop   stay   end   finish   pause   quit

bookcase   book   story   sentence   word   letter

right   correct   true   good   honest   proper

walk   run   move   roll   hurry   chase

How many letters does the last word in this sentence have?
Can you walk when you are in a hurry, or do you have to run?

Devour is to is to eat quickly and enthusiastically, like you're really hungry, but it can also be applied to reading and other activities.

Crown refers to the branches and leaves at the top of the tree.

Lesson 99

nibble   bite   chew   chomp   munch   **devour**

laugh   smile   mouth   frown   wink   grin

leaf   twig   branch   stick   trunk   **crown**

cool   chilly   cold   frozen   icy   artic

When you eat peas, do you nibble them or munch them?

If a tree has a crown, does it also have a head?

If warm is the opposite of cold, what is the opposite of hot?

Require could be necessary, like you're required to put your socks on first because they don't fit over your shoes, or compulsory, like you're required to do this because I'm making you.

Lesson 100

see   look   watch   search   view   discover

stare   glare   nice   good   kind   helpful

ask   question   invite   beg   whine   **require**

warm   hot   toasty   heat   simmer   melting

Which words on this page are good, and which are bad?

Can a happy person glare?

About This Book

Brian Murray is an IT consultant, engineer, project manager and manager who lives in Chicago with his wife and two children.

In 2011, Brian discovered gifted and talented programs about 8 weeks before the test. At this time, there was very little information about the content of this mystery test, how to prepare for it, and what material was available. A home grown crash course did the trick, but just barely, and did nothing to prepare the child for a 1st grade class that uses 3rd grade curriculum.

This Pre-K Phonics course resulted from research into the skills that the tests are measuring, the behavior of parents whose children are top readers, strategies to make a strong reader without being one of these parents, and solid preparation for what lies ahead. Then end goal is not a child who uses words like 'mull' are 'burr' in a sentence, but a child who becomes a stronger thinker by being exposed to a discussion using 'mull' and 'burr'. This can't happen without a parent who raises the bar on home discussion, and therefore this book is as much about training the parent as training the child.

www.getyourchildintogat.com chronicles these efforts from the beginning. The blog contains the latest list of the academic skill set for the child and the coaching skill set for the parent. The most popular page of this website lists the curriculum available for teaching children cognitive skills and academic skills. Among the recommendations are the 4 books authored by Brian Murray that close gaps in the list, including Pre-K Phonics for verbal skills and Shape Size Color Count for quantitative sills, as well as the Test Prep Math for both skill sets for 2nd to 4th grade. The website lists other publishers for everything else.

Nights and weekends, Brian devises and tests approaches to teaching cognitive skills and coaches a few children and a lot of parents.

Made in the USA
Middletown, DE
19 December 2017